HELP FOR MAKING DIFFICULT DECISIONS

Reverend Eamon Tobin

One Liguori Drive
Liguori, Missouri 63057
(314) 464-2500

Imprimi Potest:
John F. Dowd, C.SS.R.
Provincial, St. Louis Province
Redemptorist Fathers

Imprimatur:
+ Edward J. O'Donnell
Vicar General, Archdiocese of St. Louis

ISBN 0-89243-267-5

Acknowledgements

This booklet is in many ways a joint effort in that the final manuscript represents the views of many people. While I have learned much about the art of discernment from actually practicing it myself, I have also learned much from the wisdom of others.

I am very grateful to many people who read earlier drafts of this manuscript and offered countless suggestions in both style and content. I hope each of these readers will recognize some of his or her contributions in this final edition. I am particularly grateful to Father Thomas Green, S.J., whose book on discernment, *Weeds Among the Wheat,* was a constant inspiration and companion to me along the way. Finally, I am grateful to Jo Ann Perry, who not only patiently typed and retyped the various drafts of the booklet, but offered me invaluable support and assistance in ways too numerous to mention.

Table of Contents

b) Identify potential obstacles
c) Seek out a good counselor

Step Three: Bring the Gathered Data to Prayer
Step Four: Make a Decision
Step Five: Live With the Decision
Step Six: Act On the Decision
Step Seven: Confirm the Decision

Introduction

"Should I marry John?"

"Every time I pray, I'm only conscious of how unhappy I am in my marriage."

"I'm really unhappy in my present career. Should I change to something less lucrative but more fulfilling?"

"Should I go back to school?"

Decisions, decisions, decisions. . . . Life is full of decisions, big and small. It has been said that we are the sum total of our choices. When we make a decision, we are writing another line in the script of our lives; hence we can see the importance of making good choices. As followers of Christ, we want to make decisions that are in accord with our Father's will so that we may grow as human and spiritual persons and walk the paths that he created for us to travel. On the other hand, if we refuse to follow God's will, our choices may not only lead us away from God but can also lead to personal diminishment and death. Just before the Israelites entered the Promised Land, Moses called them together and tried to impress on them the importance of good choices. He said to them: "Here, then, I have today set before you life and prosperity, death and doom. If you obey the commandments of the LORD, your God . . . you will live and grow numerous, and the LORD, your God, will bless you. . . . If, however, you turn away your hearts and will not listen . . . you will certainly perish" (Deuteronomy 30:15-18).

When it comes to decision making, most of us would like to be able to pick up the phone, call heaven and say, "God, this is one of your friends here on earth. I'm faced with these choices; what do you want me to do?" Even though no such direct line to God exists, that is not to say that no divine guidance is available to us as we journey through life. As Christians we believe that because the Holy Spirit lives in our hearts (see 1 Corinthians 6:19) we can indeed come to some understanding of the things of God (see 1 Corinthians 2:10) and come to a good sense of his truth for our lives. Before he left this earth to return to his Father, Jesus promised the apostles that he would send the Holy Spirit to them. He said:

> I will ask the Father
> and he will give you another Paraclete —
> to be with you always:
> the Spirit of truth (John 14:16-17).

One of the key roles of God's Spirit in our lives is to act as our Divine Counselor.

When we read the Acts of the Apostles (sometimes called the Gospel of the Holy Spirit), we see evidence of the Holy Spirit guiding the early Church. One of the best known examples of this is the Council of Jerusalem, convened to deal with the problem of whether Gentiles ought to adopt Jewish laws and customs in order to become Christians (see Acts 15). In a letter that came from the leaders of the Council, we have the words, "It is the decision of the Holy Spirit, and ours too" (see Acts 15:28). Such a statement clearly shows how aware the early Church was of the Holy Spirit's guiding presence. In Acts 13:2, we read, "On one occasion, while they were engaged in the liturgy of the Lord and were fasting, the Holy Spirit spoke to them: 'Set apart Barnabas and Saul for me to do the work for which I have called them.' " In Acts 16:6, we read, "They next traveled through Phrygia and Galatian territory because they had been prevented by the Holy Spirit from preaching the message in the province of Asia." Here it should be pointed out that there is a real danger in what has been called "pipeline spirituality" ("the Holy Spirit told me to . . . " as opposed to "I had a sense that the Spirit was saying to me . . . "). This danger did not seem to exist among the early Christians; they fully expected the Holy Spirit to guide them in the big and small decisions of life. But it may exist in today's world. The same Holy Spirit who guided Jesus in his ministry and who was so obviously present in the life of the early Church lives within us seeking to guide us as he guided the early Christians.

Discernment is normally applied to situations where there is ambiguity, where it is not clear what God wants from us in a particular situation. For example, a person might wonder, "Should I quit my job, a particular relationship, or ministry?" The discernment process involves exploring the possible options available to us and then praying to discover which option is possible for us to pursue at this time and which will also contribute to our human and spiritual growth.

When it comes to decision making, the reason Christians need to go through a discernment process is because the Holy Spirit is not the only voice that seeks our attention. The voices of the world, the flesh, and the devil also seek to influence the direction of our lives. Saint John tells us that it is not every voice that we can trust (see 1 John 4:1). Therefore, we are faced with the challenge of distinguishing the voice of God from the voices that are not of God.

Even a cursory reading of modern-day literature on discernment helps us to see rather quickly that the discernment process can be a rather complex matter. This is due basically to our lack of self-knowledge, our inordinate attachments which lead to a lack of inner freedom, our tendency toward self-indulgence, our great inclination to make God say "yes" to what we ourselves want, and, of course, our lack of experiential knowledge of God. Yet none of this should block us because with the Holy Spirit on our side and with a willingness to learn through reading, dialoguing with other mature Christians, and especially through doing, we will be pleasantly surprised to see how quickly we will grow in our ability to recognize and discern the voice of God.

These pages, then, are meant to serve as a "Beginner's Guide" for those who wish to grow more in the art of discernment or decision making. Those who read them carefully will become more deeply aware of the conditions that can help or hinder them in the search for God's will in their daily lives.

In this booklet, the words *discernment* and *Christian decision-making* are used interchangeably. Discernment is the gift and art of discovering God's will in the concrete situations of life. Thus, discernment has a divine and a human dimension to it. It is one of the gifts of the Holy Spirit (see 1 Corinthians 12:10) and therefore we ought to pray often for it. It is an art that we learn basically by doing — by trial and error. The human dimension of discernment involves doing all that we can to dispose ourselves to hearing God's voice. By becoming aware of the obstacles (Chapter One) and helps (Chapter Two) and by following certain guidelines to overcome the obstacles in concrete situations (Chapter Three), we will be growing in the human dimension of the discernment process.

Since there are many different procedures for making decisions, before you study the method proposed here you should try to get in touch with your present technique of decision making. For example, if you were faced with a decision about changing jobs, relocating, or responding to an invitation to become involved in a particular ministry, ask yourself what process you would go through. Would you write down the pros and cons of the alternatives available to you? Would you seek the advice of other people? Or would you usually go with your gut feeling without analyzing any pros and cons? Once you have reviewed your own discernment process, you can use this booklet to pick and choose the ideas that might help you to become better discerners of God's will, better decision-makers.

I.
Obstacles to Discernment

"Since the mysterious voice of the Spirit is not the only voice we hear but comes to us accompanied by the tumultuous sounds of our own conflicting impulses and the clamoring of the entire creation, it is essential for us to be able to discern the presence of the Spirit in order to choose to say 'yes' to him" (Graham Green). As we seek to learn the art of discernment, we must become aware of the other voices or spirits that compete with the voice of the Holy Spirit for our attention. For the Christian, this practical question must be asked: "Is the Lord present and leading me in this situation or decision, or am I just doing my own thing, being duped by the evil one?"

The three main voices that compete with the voice of the Spirit for our attention are the voices of the world, the flesh, and the devil.

The World. Some Christian preachers today look upon the world in an almost totally negative way. While there is, of course, much wrong in the world, it will always be basically good since it was created good by God. In our own day we have many examples of how the Spirit of God can move in our world, even outside of Christian circles and religious institutions. The movements for social justice, women's rights, disarmament, sharing food and resources with starving peoples, and many other concerns are all examples of how the Spirit of God moves in our world.

But all is not well with the world. Our world is still seriously wounded by the Fall, and it has not responded very well to the redemptive and healing work of Christ. Insofar as this unredeemed part of the world influences our thinking and behavior, it will present a serious obstacle to our efforts to hear and to follow the voice of Jesus, the Good Shepherd (see John 10:15-16). The unredeemed part of the world does not seek to hear the voice of Jesus but seeks the vices of excessive pleasure, power, and success. The world's spirit urges us not to follow the voice of Jesus; it urges us to do our own thing, even if that means using abortion to deal with an unplanned pregnancy, divorce as a way out of a bothersome marriage, mercy killing as a way to deal with pain and old age, or religious activities as a way to escape family responsibilities.

This is the "world" Jesus refused to pray for as the hour of his Passion approached (see John 17:9). This is the "world" that Saint John spoke about when he wrote,

> If anyone loves the world,
> the Father's love has no place in him (1 John 2:15).

This is the world — of which we are a part because we live in it — that will be a great hindrance to us in our efforts to make godly decisions.

Jesus tells us that no person can "serve two masters" (see Matthew 6:24). He also warns us that preoccupation with the worries of the world and the lure of riches will indeed choke off the voice of God (see Matthew 13:22). Because the voice of the world that is anti-God is so strong, subtle, and pervasive in our society, we can be sure that it has infected our ways of thinking and acting much more than we realize. In turn, such infection diminishes our ability to hear the Word of God and do his will. For the Christian, the daily challenge is to live in the world, to recognize and cooperate with the movement of God's Spirit in the world, to retain an unselfish love for all persons, and yet not to be contaminated by the spirit of the world that is not of God.

The Flesh. In this context, the word *flesh* does not mean our physical body and its legitimate desires for pleasure. Like the world, God created our bodies and said that they were very good. Therefore, our bodies are good, but it is essential that we learn to appreciate our bodies and their legitimate desire for sensual pleasure. *Flesh* connotes that unredeemed part of us that desires to indulge itself by being its own master and does not want to submit to the Lordship of Christ or to the direction of his Holy Spirit. It is that sinful, wounded, flawed part of us that causes us to do the evil we hate and fails to carry out the good that we want to do (see Romans 7:14-21). It is that part of us that is at home with and desires the values and allurements of the world. It includes conscious and unconscious fears, anxieties, insecurities, compulsions, and inordinate attachments. It includes the tendencies in us toward any or all of the seven capital sins: pride, anger, envy, greed, lust, laziness, and gluttony. Finally, it is that part of us that does not *really* believe or trust in God the Father's overwhelming love and care for us personally.

When it comes to hearing God's voice and direction for our lives, we need to be very aware of the *flesh* dimension of our beings that can wield such conscious and unconscious power over us and draw us away from yielding to the Holy Spirit, especially the Spirit who sometimes calls us to follow him in directions we would prefer not to travel (see John 21:18). This strange and often unconscious dimension of the self makes us quite vulnerable as we try to make God want what we want when it comes to matters of discernment. We say we love God and the things of God, and indeed we do. We also love other things, which is good. The problem arises when we love other things *more than* we love God. Our inordinate attachment to these other things may not only deafen us to the voice of God but will also diminish the *inner freedom* which we need for saying "yes" to the call or voice of God. Hence, as we shall see later, a very important part of our prayer during a discernment process is praying for the grace to be detached from our own desires and attachments and for the grace to want to know and do God's will more than anything else.

The Devil. Saint Paul tells us that in our efforts to follow Christ we are not just struggling against flesh and blood but also against supernatural powers of darkness (see Ephesians 6:11-13). Thus the devil is a third voice or obstacle that we need to be aware of as we seek to hear the voice of God for our lives. The author of Genesis tells us that he is the "most cunning" of all the creatures created by God (see Genesis 3:1). Jesus calls the devil the "father of lies" (see John 8:44). Saint Paul says that in order to deceive us the devil is willing to disguise himself as an "angel of light" (see 2 Corinthians 11:14). From all this we can see that we have a formidable and sophisticated enemy in the devil when we are seeking the truth. Only the foolish would ignore his reality and his ability to trip us up in our efforts to hear and follow God's voice.

We need to be aware that one minute God may be at work in our lives revealing his truth to us, and the very next minute the devil may actually trick us into moving against the ways of God. We have a very concrete example of all this in the Caesarea Philippi incident (see Matthew 16:13-23), where one moment we have God the Father revealing to Peter the true identity of Jesus (verse 17) and the next moment Peter is told that Satan is using him to block Jesus from following his Father's will (verse 23).

Finally, while we cannot blame the devil for our errant ways, we need to be aware that the devil usually attacks us in those areas of our lives where we are most vulnerable spiritually, physically, mentally, or emotionally. Again we can see the need to be aware of our vulnerability to excessive needs, inordinate attachments and compulsions, and for our need to pray to God for protection against the wiles and deceptions of Satan (see Ephesians 6:13).

Exercise

1. In what specific ways did this chapter help you to be aware of potential obstacles to good decision making?
2. What do you think are some concrete obstacles that you would have to struggle with in a decision making situation? For example, are you inclined to be impulsive when it comes to decisions?
3. Would you be inclined to take *too much* stock in what other people think?

II.
Helps for Discernment

Discernment, as was seen, is both a gift (the divine dimension) and an art (the human dimension) in which we can grow. Insofar as discernment is a gift, we can never earn it. All we can do is pray for it and dispose ourselves the best we can for its reception. This chapter will provide the necessary help for proper discernment. It will identify some key dispositions that should help us to grow in this gift that God gives to all of us in seed form when we receive the Sacrament of Baptism.

Living a God-centered Life. The most important disposition that we need to develop in the art of discovering and doing God's will is seeking to live a life that is God-centered. Father Thomas Green calls this disposition the ''blank-check'' attitude (*Weeds Among the Wheat,* p. 55). We give God permission to ask anything of us and to lead us wherever he decides. While few, if any, of us totally live the ''blank-check'' attitude in relationship to God, we must at least — if we are to grow in the art of discernment — be praying people who take God seriously and are genuinely concerned with his involvement in our lives.

Whether we are aware of it or not, most of our day-to-day decisions *flow out of* what is sometimes called our basic life decision or orientation. Therefore it is very important for us to ask ourselves now and again: ''What is *the* basic orientation or central project of my life? How is this orientation related to my day-to-day decisions?'' For example, if the basic orientation or central project of our life is material gain, a particular friendship, attainment of power, pleasure, or sports, then all of our little and not-so-little choices will be made out of this orientation. For Jesus, the basic orientation or central project of his life was his relationship with his Father and following his will:

Doing the will of him who sent me
and bringing his work to completion
is my food (John 4:23).

In light of the above, we can see how critical it is for us to be in touch with the relationships or concerns that mean the most to us because it is such relationships and concerns that are consciously or unconsciously determining our daily choices. For the Christian, the most important basic disposition needed to help in discovering God's will in specific situations is a basic life attitude that seeks not only to discover God's will but also seeks to carry out his will, whatever it may cost. The attitude that says, "I am going to pray to discover God's will and then decide if I want to do it," is not the ideal basic attitude needed to discover God's will. We ought, instead, to pray, "Incline my heart according to your will, O Lord, and make pleasing you the all-consuming passion of my life."

Personal Knowledge of God and His Ways. Father Thomas Green writes: "One might desire to do God's will but have no idea how to discover it. He or she might have good desires but not solid knowledge of God or his ways. . . . If I do not know you, I can scarcely do what pleases you" (*Weeds Among the Wheat,* p. 61). The knowledge of God that we are talking about here is not knowledge *about* God but personal or experiential knowledge, the knowledge one has of someone after living with and loving another person for years. Spouses who have developed a very loving relationship with each other through the years learn to know each other's likes and dislikes. This, in contrast to an acquaintance or even a son or daughter who lack that intimate knowledge. So a second key disposition needed to grow in discernment is growth in a personal relationship with God.

For Christians, the primary way to come to a knowledge of God is through meditation on the life of Jesus, his values and his attitudes; thus we come to know the heart of God, for Jesus is *the* revelation of God. The less personal knowledge we have of God and his ways, the more we will have to depend on another person (sometimes called a co-discerner) who has a more mature relationship with God. What we most need to know is God's unconditional love for us. This experiential knowledge of his love will enable us to face ourselves, our sins and attachments — anything and everything that prevents us from recognizing and following God's will. Also, it is only trust in his loving care that will eventually free us to let go of anything that might block us from following God's direction for our lives.

Genuine Openness to God. This is the third key disposition needed for growth in discernment. One may be very pious and pray a lot and yet be locked into a narrow understanding of God and his ways. For example, the Pharisees had such preconceived ideas of how God ought to manifest himself that they couldn't recognize him in the person of Jesus (see John 8:13-59 and John 9:39-41). Our God, who is total mystery, must never be put into our human boxes. God is always mysterious (see Isaiah 55:8-9 and Romans 11:33-36), often surprising (see Luke 15:21-24), and sometimes disturbing (see Luke 14:25-33). True openness to God and his ways is a gift that we ought to pray for often.

Self-Knowledge. Spiritual masters have always said that a healthy self-knowledge is very important for growth in the spiritual life and that, of course, includes growth in the area of discernment. Self-knowledge involves being in touch with one's thoughts, feelings, and actions. We must be in touch with our basic orientation, the people and things (our human and material treasures), our hang-ups, as well as the driving forces and the social conditioning in our lives. Particularly, we need to be in touch with our feelings. Feelings, the affective level of our being, are the raw material of our experience with God, a primary place where the tiny whispering voice of God comes to us (see 1 Kings 19:13).

Another important dimension of self-knowledge needed for good discernment is the awareness of what might be called excessive needs or compulsions or what some of the spiritual masters call "inordinate attachments." The reason we need to be aware of these areas of our lives is because these are the things that most diminish the inner freedom we always need in saying "yes" to God's beckoning call. Some examples might be helpful here. If we have an excessive need to be accepted by people or have a great fear of rejection, then we may find it very hard to hear the Lord calling us to do something that may lead some people to criticize us, such as giving up the weekly Friday evening party in order to join a Bible study group. As alluded to earlier, we can be sure that the evil one will be working overtime in this vulnerable area of our life, which in this case is our fear of rejection.

If we have an inordinate attachment to things, we will most likely find it difficult to hear the Lord call us to simplify our lifestyle. The case of the rich, young man in the Gospel (see Luke 18:18-30) is a perfect example of someone who thought he was completely open to God's will. Then Jesus pointed out to him an inordinate attachment in his life. Unfortunately, the young man did not have the inner freedom to let go of something in his life that had become a big obstacle to a closer relationship with the Lord.

If we have an excessive need to be right or in control, then we may find it very difficult to hear or obey the Lord's call to ask a certain person's forgiveness or to yield control over some area of our life, such as the leadership of a certain group or project. Excessive needs or inordinate attachments are a difficult area of our lives, so we need to be gentle and not forceful with ourselves as we work on them. We ought to take consolation from the fact that even Jesus, in Gethsemane, had to struggle to detach himself from his love of life so that he could be free to embrace the cruel death that was a part of his Father's plan for him.

Reflective Living. Any person serious about growing in the gift and art of discernment must develop a reflective attitude toward his or her own life. The Scriptures tell us that Mary reflected on the events of her life (see Luke 2:19 and 2:51). We also know that for Jesus, "quiet time" or "desert time" was a very important part of his life (see Mark 6:46, Luke 4:42 and 6:12). He urged his apostles "to take time off" and come aside into a quiet place (see Mark 6:31). Down through the ages, our spiritual tradition tells us that discernment of spirits is impossible for the person who has little or no appreciation of silence and reflection. Without regular periods of reflective silence in the presence of God, we may fail to grow in self-knowledge, we will be out of touch with our feelings and inner urgings, and, worst of all, we will become people who are driven and controlled by our excessive needs, compulsions, and inordinate attachments. The noisy crowd will become our guide.

Many people in our Western culture have little appreciation for silence and reflective living. The emphasis is on doing, achieving, and producing. There is a second and perhaps deeper reason why we dislike silence. In the silence we will meet and be confronted by our inner demons: pride, covetousness, lust, anger, our need to be right and in control, and numerous other faults. It takes courage to face the shadowy or less attractive sides of ourselves. But if we don't, we will be choosing to live not a Spirit-led life but a life where we are slaves to our inner demons.

How might one spend periods of reflective silence? The following is one model which has three steps.

1. *Pray for Guidance and Strength*. Become aware of the loving presence of God. Know in faith (if you can't feel it) that God loves you unconditionally. It is the personal knowledge that you are loved unconditionally that enables you to look at the dark sides of life. Then pray to the Holy Spirit for his guidance and strength. For instance, you can pray: "Holy Spirit, help me to see the last few hours (days, weeks) as *you* would want me to see them. Since I cannot zero in on every detail or event of these hours, please help me to reflect on the event or encounter that *you* want me to focus on.''

2. *Reflect on a Particular Event.* In the loving and peaceful presence of God, allow a particular event or encounter to come before your mental TV screen. As you look at yourself in that situation, try to be in touch with what was going on within you. What thoughts, feelings, attitudes, and behaviors dominated? Another way to look at the past hours, days, months, would be to ask, ''To what extent have the past hours been 'we-hours' (lived with the mind and heart of Christ) as opposed to 'me-hours' (lived in a self-centered way)?''

For example, ''Did I greet people, eat my meals, drive to work, and recreate in a Christlike manner (Christ and I at work)? Or did I allow a bad mood to dominate my behavior at home, in the office, in the morning and evening traffic, and so on?'' This is not to suggest that in order to be a good Christian one must be consciously thinking of Christ at all times. But it does suggest that one try to walk through one's days with the mind and heart of Christ, behaving in a Christlike way. Growth in this area will demand *constant effort* and cooperation with the grace of God. Here again you must be gentle with yourselves and not demand too much progress in a short time.

3. *Offer Prayers of Thanks, Repentance, Healing, and Petition.* Having spent some time reflecting on some event(s) or encounter(s) in your life, now speak to your Father about the blessings and sorrows of the day and your good and not-so-good responses to these events.

For the blessings of the day, give thanks. Naming and giving thanks to God for your blessings is one concrete way to deepen your awareness of God's presence and love in your life. Also give thanks for the times you manifested positive and loving attitudes and behaviors, for the times you recognized the Spirit's promptings and responded positively.

For the negative and unloving attitudes and behaviors, for the times you believed or felt the Lord was asking something of you and you failed to respond, repent and ask for his mercy and for the grace to do better in the hours and days ahead.

For attitudes and behaviors that reveal not so much your sinfulness but your woundedness and tiredness, ask for healing and strength.

For the help and strength you need to continue your desire and efforts to hear God's voice and do his will in all things, make prayers of petition.

Ideally, each day should have built into it a brief reflective pause moment (an R.P.M., as one person called it). You might do an R.P.M. on your way home from work in your car or in the subway. You might do it when jogging, when in the shower, as a family before dinner, or as you get into bed at night time. And if you *really* feel ambitious, you might try on occasion (once a week or month) to take longer periods of time to stand aside and look at the general flow of your life and seek the movement of God's Spirit. The underlying goal in all this is to seek to do God's will in all things. Commitment to such an exercise should be a tremendous help as you strive to become hearers and doers of God's will.

Exercise

1. What are some of the things that help you to hear and to follow God's voice?
2. Which of the dispositions mentioned in this Chapter is missing most from your life?
3. In what ways could you make that disposition a part of your life?

III.
Discernment Guidelines for Particular Situations

Having looked at the conditions that may hinder our discernment and the helps at hand to overcome them, we now consider certain guidelines that should help us to discover God's will regarding particular decisions in our lives. For example, we may wonder if it is God's will for us to change jobs, abandon a relationship, get married to a particular person, become involved with or discontinue a particular church ministry. All of these are examples of important decisions that would greatly affect our lives and should not be made without much reflection and prayer.

We know, of course, that there is no easy ABC recipe to help us to discover God's will with absolute certainty. Nevertheless, as beginners we all need some concrete guidelines to get us started. Then as we grow in the art of discernment, we will develop our own unique approach.

Step One: Formulate a Proposition. The first step is to formulate a clear statement about what we are trying to discern or decide. For example, "Should I quit my present job?" "Should I terminate my relationship with so-and-so?" "Should I return to school?" "Should I attend the Lenten Renewal Series in my parish?" From the beginning and right through this process, we ought to ask the Lord to reveal to us his truth and to give us the inner freedom to carry it out. As we go through the decision making process, we need to do all that we can to be conscious of the attachments and the needs in us that may block us from listening for and carrying out God's will.

Step Two: Gather the Relevant Data and Input. This step involves three parts.

a) Reflect on the pros and cons of available alternatives. As we do this, we should be as creative as possible. For example, there may be more options available to us than just quitting or continuing a job or relationship. Perhaps it is possible for us to continue in a job or relationship but work toward (or even demand) some definite changes. Having listed some of the alternatives or options available to us, we could then jot down the pros and cons of each alternative. In doing this it is often suggested that we jot down all of the pros and cons we are aware of, the ones that seem to flow from the Spirit and from the flesh. It is important that we take our time with this list and that we try to make it when we are peaceful and open to the Spirit. If we make the list hurriedly during one sitting, we are likely to be in contact only with what is dominating our consciousness at that time. If we make it over a period of days, then we have a better chance of being in touch with a fuller range of motives within ourselves. (See *Moving in the Spirit,* Richard Hauser, p. 71, for a practical example of this.)

As we begin to reflect on the pros and cons of each alternative, we need to pay special attention to primary responsibilities and commitments, especially to God and family and perhaps to co-workers and the larger community, depending on the particular situation we are trying to discern. On looking at the possible alternatives, we also need to consider how each alternative fits into the flow of our lives up to this point. God sometimes invites us to a task that differs entirely from our present line of work. In that case we should be able to recognize that our special abilities and life experiences are in some way a preparation for this new calling. If we cannot see any connection between the talent needed for our past endeavors and the talent needed for this future project, perhaps we have good reason to question whether God is actually calling us to this new endeavor.

This is not to say that God may not sometimes call us in a direction which seems to have little or no connection with the flow of our lives up until now. Indeed he may. What must be emphasized here is that if that happens, one needs to do a lot of prayerful checking in order to be as sure as possible that it is God who is doing the calling.

b) Identify potential obstacles. This especially concerns matters that may hinder our inner freedom, both from within and without (see Chapter One). What excessive needs, attachments, and compulsions might be preventing our hearing God's Word and doing his will? For example, to what extent are we attached to one particular alternative? How free are we to embrace any alternative or direction if we believe it is God's will for us? Are there external obstacles? For example, to what extent do we fear the reaction of other people to a particular alternative or direction?

Being willing to name and admit obstacles to our inner freedom demands a *rare* kind of honesty, courage, and patience. We need honesty to face up to and acknowledge the obstacles. We need courage to be willing to let go of them. And we need patience as we wait for God to help us surrender our inordinate attachments. This part of the discernment process is very, very critical. It must be honestly faced and dealt with or we run the great and sad risk of choosing our own compulsions, attachments, or likes, and then thinking we have discovered and chosen God's will.

c) Seek out a good counselor. We need the help of a wise spiritual person. Saint Ignatius tells us that the devil loves secrecy, whereas God blesses openness. Father Thomas Green has said: "It is undoubtedly true that he who listens *only* to himself has a fool for a hearer," and usually he who guides himself has a fool for a guide. The Bible advises us to seek counsel from every wise person and warns us not to think lightly of any advice that can be useful" (see Tobit 4:18). In light of all this, it would seem that somewhere in the decision-making process we would do well to seek the input of a wise spiritual director or friend, preferably one who knows us well. This step is particularly important for people who are not mature in the Lord's ways. The role of the spiritual director will not be to tell us what to do but to act as a co-discerner, one who helps us to make our own sound judgments about God's Word to us. In the end we must make our own choices and be responsible before God for our own decisions.

Step Three: Bring the Gathered Data to Prayer. This means that we pray over the various alternatives available to us and the potential obstacles that may diminish our interior freedom and get in the way of our hearing God's Word and doing his will. Our first order of business might be to pray for the grace of inner freedom or detachment from the likes and dislikes we spontaneously feel about the options available to us. In some situations it may take weeks and even months of prayer, plus the support of a spiritual guide, to help us arrive at a point of inner freedom and detachment. But the more we surrender our likes and attachments and begin to experience spiritual freedom, the more we will be able to look at the persons and circumstances of our situation with the eyes of God. Gradually God frees us from looking at our situation with our jaundiced eyes. The more inner freedom we experience, the more space there is for God to enter our hearts, which in turn will empower us to move with the Spirit of God. In short, we must allow God to make us free so that we can find out in freedom what God is asking of us.

Having attained, through the grace of God, a good degree of inner freedom, we now begin to pray about the various options available to us. We will take one option and spend some days reflecting and praying about it, noting our inner reactions and feelings to the option. As we pray we might want to imagine ourselves living out a particular alternative in its details. We might also want to note in a journal the spontaneous likes, dislikes, prejudices, and fears we have about a particular option. We should note which alternative gives us the most peace and sense of God's presence, joy, and strength. The option that consistently fills us with the presence of God's peace and joy over a period of time is most likely God's will for us.

Note that in all of this the decision made is not primarily based on the pros and cons of a particular option (the data gathered in Step Two) but on the inner feelings we experienced as we prayed about such options. Deciding on a particular option based on reasons for or against (Step Two) without the prayer dimension (Step Three) would result in a *prudent decision,* but not a discerning one, in the Christian understanding of that term. The heart of Christian discernment is not the intellectual activity of weighing the pros and cons of available options, but rather it is the act of bringing the available options to prayer and seeing which option gives us the greatest sense of God's presence, peace, and joy. "Discernment is not just a conviction of the head based on sound reasons and arguments. It is like a sixth sense for the things of God" (Ernest Larkin).

To help us in our prayer during this part of the discernment process, Saint Ignatius suggests three imaginative exercises. First, we should consider what advice we would give to another person faced with the same situation. It is interesting to see how clear our situation becomes when we picture someone else facing the decision. Second, we can imagine being on our deathbed and then asking what we would then wish to have chosen. Third, we should picture ourselves standing before God on the last day and then consider what decision in the present matter we would wish to have made. The above exercises will help us to distance ourselves from our decisions and to look at them with greater objectivity.

Step Four: Make a Decision. Sometimes we may come to a clear and peaceful decision without too much struggle. At other times the right direction is not at all clear. There may be good arguments for or against the various alternatives available to us. At this point, Father Thomas Green, one of the best teachers in discernment, has a helpful question for us. When people seek his advice about making a difficult choice, he usually asks them how they feel about it when they are most at peace — when they are "at prayer and quiet (not emotional) and most open to whatever the Lord wants" (*Opening to God,* p. 51). Often the doubt or confusion that we are experiencing arises when we are reflecting on the question or issue *outside* of prayer, so it is very important that we make a distinction between what we feel is right when we are in prayer, at peace, and most open to God's will and what we feel when we are reflecting outside of prayer and are not at peace.

What if we experience no real peace about the various options available to us? We can do one of two things. We can postpone the decision, or we can choose the least troublesome option as we see it. Saint Ignatius counsels us not to decide when in doubt, so if time permits, it is best to continue praying until we experience God's peace about a particular option. But in the end we must decide; for not to decide is ultimately to decide. We are responsible before God for the choices we make along the journey of life.

We must also realize that the direction or option we choose may not be the most attractive one available to us or the one we most desired. In fact, we may embrace a particular option with tears. We may decide through prayer, for example, to return to a marriage situation that in the past caused us much pain. However, such initial tears of sadness often give way to tears of joy (see 2 Corinthians 7:8-13).

Step Five: Live With the Decision. Once we come to a decision, it is good to live with it for a while before we actually act on what was decided. This is particularly important if we tend to be impulsive. Father Richard Hauser, S.J., tells us why it is good for us to sit with our decision for a while before acting on it. He writes: "If the decision is truly from the Lord, usually our minds will find more reasons to support it, our wills will be held toward the decision and the feeling of consolation will accompany our thoughts on our decision. This drawing of mind, will, and feeling occurs as frequently outside of prayer as during prayer. Often we are simply struck with the fact that what we have decided is right for ourselves. Since this conviction arises spontaneously in us with no preparation on our part, we know that we are being held toward the decision by the Holy Spirit and not by our own will'' (*Moving in the Spirit,* p. 76).

Step Six: Act On the Decision. Having lived in peace with our decision for some appropriate length of time, the next step in the process is to act on it. This may seem obvious, but in some situations this sixth step may be the most difficult one of the whole process, for it may involve letting go of something or someone to which/whom we are still quite attached. Our prayer here should involve asking the Holy Spirit to give us the power and courage we need to act on that which we believe to be God's will for our lives. Often the encouragement of a spiritual director or friends can also help us to carry out a decision that we believe is God's will.

Step Seven: Confirm the Decision. As we begin to act on the choice made, we await God's confirmation of it. Father Matthew Linn, S.J., tells us that ''the final test for hearing God's will is whether living it out brings life to me and to others. Is this choice the way I can best give and receive love?'' In addition, as we seek to live out God's choice for us, we can expect to feel God's peace within. Yet this is not to say that we won't have days when we experience struggle and conflict and wonder if we really did the right thing. Such difficult days and feelings are normal and do not necessarily prove that we made a wrong decision. If the decision made brings us life and gives us a sense of peace, especially when we concentrate on the presence of God, then we have two good reasons to believe that we acted in accord with God's will. On the other hand, if our chosen direction gives us little peace or bears but little fruit, then there is every reason to wonder whether we actually followed God's will for us. By withholding a sense of rightness or ongoing peace about our decision, God will indicate to us that our decision was a poor one and consequently a wrong one.

There is one final question: What if we discover later that we made the wrong decision? First of all, we ought to be very consoled by the fact that we made a sincere effort to seek God's will. Remember that discernment is not just a gift but an art that we learn through trial and error. The only real mistake is the one we keep repeating and learn nothing from. The Lord doesn't ask that we always be right; he asks only that we try to be honest and to act out of the best understanding we have of a particular situation. Then, too, we should be consoled when we remember God's ability to use our mistakes to his (and our) advantage. In our messy lives, God is always writing straight with crooked lines. Saint Paul offers us comforting words when he says, "We know that God makes all things work together for the good of those who love him, who have been called according to his decree" (Romans 8:28).

Not too much can be said — from a practical viewpoint — to those persons who discover that they have made a wrong decision because often a whole new set of circumstances may have arisen. For example, in a relational situation a wife or husband may have remarried or the job that one gave up may now belong to someone else. All that can be suggested is to begin the whole process again. After examination of circumstances, available options should be reviewed to see which ones can best redeem the first mistake and contribute, at the same time, to human and spiritual growth. God is so merciful and creative that often he teaches us the most valuable of lessons in the detours of life's journey.

To conclude: You must never become discouraged in your efforts to arrive at discernment. At some point you may begin to think: "Oh, this is so complex and intricate; I don't think I can put it all into practice." Others have felt the same way. What they did was to pick out the parts which they thought they could handle at that time and which they knew would enrich their present method of decision-making. The parts that were too complex or too nuanced for them were just put aside until they themselves became more mature in this area of the spiritual life. You can do the same with this booklet. Use what you feel you are ready for at this time and leave the rest, remaining open to further growth in this important dimension of the Christian life.

> Choose life, then, that you and your descendants may live, by loving the LORD, your God, heeding his voice, and holding fast to him. For that will mean life for you (Deuteronomy 30:19-20).

> Probe me, O God, and know my heart;
> try me, and know my thoughts;
> See if my way is crooked,
> and lead me in the way of old (Psalm 139:23-24).

Exercise

1. Do you use any of the seven steps explained in this chapter when you are trying to make a decision?
2. Which of the above steps would enhance your present method of decision making?

NOTE: The author would very much appreciate any feedback his readers may wish to offer. "Has this booklet helped you in any way?" "Were certain areas unclear to you?" "Are there other helpful techniques — experienced by you — that were not mentioned in this booklet?" Please write to Reverend Eamon Tobin in care of Liguori Publications, Books and Pamphlet Department, One Liguori Drive, Liguori, Missouri 63057.